PASTA

SUMPTUOUS SAUCES, SALADS
AND BAKES FOR CREATIVE COOKING

REBO
PRODUCTIONS

Contents

Introduction

Pasta in its various forms, but essentially a paste or dough made from flour and water, plays a role in many cuisines. However, it is at its most prominent and versatile in Italian and Chinese cooking.

Pasta and Oriental-style noodles come in a variety of types, to suit different uses and tastes. Besides the common 'white' and wholemeal varieties, Italian pasta is also readily available flavoured with spinach and tomato, fresh or dried and with or without the addition of egg. Wheat noodles and egg noodles also come fresh or dried, but rice noodles and the fine transparent cellophane noodles, made from ground mung beans, are usually only available in dried form.

Additionally, Italian pasta comes in more than a hundred different shapes which can be used to create a whole range of exciting and wholesome dishes. Some of these shapes are especially suited to certain sauces or uses. For instance, long, round strand pasta, such as spaghetti or vermicelli, is best served with oil-based sauces, to keep the strands separate. Choose light sauces for the very fine types of strand pasta to avoid it breaking up. Long, flat pasta, such as fettuccine, tagliatelle and lasagne, suit heavier-based sauces made with cheese, eggs and/or cream. Short, tubular types of pasta, such as penne or macaroni, need a more chunky but sufficiently liquid sauce to penetrate into their hollow centres. They are excellent for baked dishes with rich meat or vegetable and cheese sauces. Other pasta shapes widely available include conchiglie (shells), fusilli, (spirals) and Farfalle (butterflies or bows), which are highly versatile. Stuffed pasta, such as ravioli, requires a delicate sauce, so as not to overwhelm the flavour of the filling. It is also good served in a light soup or stock.

Here is a selection of superior recipes for making delicious pasta dishes for every occasion. Many of these are quick and easy to make, for family meals as well as trouble-free entertaining. Some have light, vegetable-based sauces for healthy eating, while others are wickedly indulgent. Choose from classic favourites and contemporary creations, to satisfy all manner of tastes!

Chinese Chicken Soup

A delicious and filling Oriental-style pasta soup – ideal for a satisfying lunch or supper.

Preparation time: 25 minutes, plus soaking time • Cooking time: 1 hour 25 minutes • Serves: 4-6

Ingredients

25 g (1 oz) Chinese mushrooms	50 g (1¾ oz) Chinese noodles, soaked in water
6 chicken or vegetable stock cubes	350-g (12-oz) can bamboo shoots, drained
1 oven-ready chicken, weighing about 1 kg (2 lb 4 oz)	Soy sauce
200 g (7 oz) prepared fresh soup vegetables, such as onions, carrots, leeks and parsnips	Sambal oelek (Oriental chilli sauce)

Method

1

Soak the Chinese mushrooms in a bowl of water for several hours, drain, then slice into strips. Set aside.

2

Bring 2½ litres (4½ pints) water to the boil in a large saucepan and stir in the stock cubes until dissolved. Add the chicken and soup vegetables, return to the boil, then reduce the heat and simmer for about 1 hour.

3

Remove the chicken from the stock, reserving the stock. Remove the chicken flesh from the bones, discarding the skin and bones. Cut the chicken into small pieces.

4

Add the noodles and Chinese mushrooms to the soup, bring back to the boil and cook for a further 10 minutes.

5

Return the chopped chicken to the soup with the bamboo shoots and allow to heat through briefly. Stir in the soy sauce and sambal oelek to taste. Ladle into warmed soup bowls and serve.

Serving suggestion
Serve with thick slices of fresh crusty bread.

Variations
Use turkey in place of chicken. Use water chestnuts, sliced, in place of bamboo shoots.

Cook's tip
Sambal oelek is available from Oriental food stores.

Cabbage and Pasta Soup

Use homemade chicken stock, if available, as the basis of this hearty soup for maximum flavour.

Preparation time: 15 minutes • Cooking time: 35 minutes • Serves: 4

Ingredients

6 leaves white cabbage	*850 ml (1½ pints) chicken stock*
15 ml (1 tbsp) olive oil	*Salt and freshly ground black pepper*
1 clove garlic, chopped	*140 g (5 oz) small pasta shells*
1 rasher streaky bacon, cut into small dice	

Method

1

Cut the cabbage into thin strips. To do this, roll the leaves into cigar shapes and cut with a very sharp knife. Set aside.

2

Heat the olive oil in a saucepan and fry the garlic, bacon and cabbage together for 2 minutes, stirring.

3

Add the stock and season with salt and pepper. Bring to the boil, then cook over
a moderate heat for 30 minutes, stirring occasionally.

4

Add the pasta to the soup after it has been cooking for 15 minutes. Stir well.

5

Adjust the seasoning and ladle into warmed soup bowls to serve.

Serving suggestion

Serve with warm fresh bread rolls.

Variations

Use smoked bacon for a change. Use green cabbage in place of white cabbage.

Beef and Noodle Soup

Marinated beef is sliced and cooked in beef stock with noodles to make a wonderfully rich soup.

Preparation time: 10 minutes, plus 15 minutes marinating time • Cooking time: 20 minutes • Serves: 4

Ingredients

225 g (8 oz) fillet of beef	*225 g (8 oz) fresh noodles*
2.5 ml (½ tsp) chopped garlic	*A few drops of sesame oil*
1 spring onion, chopped	*700 ml (1¼ pints) beef stock*
30 ml (2 tbsp) soy sauce	*A few drops of chilli sauce*
Salt and freshly ground black pepper	*15 ml (1 tbsp) chopped fresh chives*

Method

1

Cut the beef into thin slices and place in a shallow dish. Sprinkle the chopped garlic and spring onion over the meat. Sprinkle over the soy sauce and season with salt and pepper. Set aside and leave the meat to marinate for 15 minutes.

2

Cook the noodles in a large saucepan of boiling, salted water to which a few drops of sesame oil have been added for 3-4 minutes. Rinse in cold water and set aside to drain.

3

Bring the stock to the boil in a saucepan and add the beef and the marinade. Simmer gently for 10 minutes, stirring occasionally.

4

Stir in the noodles, season with chilli sauce and simmer just long enough to heat the noodles through.

5

Ladle into warmed soup bowls and serve with chives sprinkled over the top.

Serving suggestion
Serve with thick slices of fresh bread or toast.

Variations
Use lamb in place of beef. Use chopped fresh ginger in place of garlic.

Cook's tip
A quick and easy way to chop fresh chives is to snip them using a pair of clean kitchen scissors.

Ravioli Soup

Fresh pasta rectangles are filled with Parma ham and butter then cooked in chicken stock – an elegant starter for an extra-special meal.

Preparation time: 45 minutes, plus 30 minutes resting time • Cooking time: 10 minutes • Serves: 4

Ingredients

225 g (8 oz) plain flour, sifted	*1 litre (1³/₄ pints) chicken stock*
3 eggs	*Ground nutmeg*
Salt and freshly ground black pepper	*30 ml (2 tbsp) single cream*
3 slices Parma ham, cut into very thin strips	*A sprig of fresh tarragon, leaves stripped off and cut into strips*
25 g (1 oz) butter	

Method

1
Make the pasta dough by mixing together the flour, 2 eggs and a good pinch of salt in a large bowl.
Set aside to rest for 30 minutes.

2
Roll out the pasta dough very thinly either with a rolling pin or by passing through a pasta machine, and cut into rectangles.

3
Place a little Parma ham and butter on one half of each rectangle.

4
Beat the remaining egg in a small bowl. Brush the edges of each piece of dough with the beaten egg.

5
Fold each rectangle in half to form a square and pinch the edges firmly with your fingers to seal. Either trim these squares into various shapes or decorate the edges of the squares with the prongs of a fork.

6
Bring the stock to boil in a large saucepan and season with nutmeg and salt and pepper.

7
Tip the ravioli into the stock and simmer gently for about 2-5 minutes, depending on the thickness of the ravioli.

8
Stir the cream into the soup just before serving and sprinkle over the tarragon. Ladle into warmed soup bowls and serve.

Serving suggestion
Serve with homemade melba toast or crackers.

Variations
Use smoked cooked ham in place of Parma ham. Use basil or parsley in place of tarragon.

Cook's tip
The use of cream in this soup is optional, but it gives a nice smooth taste to the stock.

Cheese, Pasta and Noodle Salad

A quick salad to make combining pasta and noodles with Roquefort and Emmenthal cheeses – ideal for summertime eating alfresco.

Preparation time: 20 minutes, plus cooling time • Cooking time: 10 minutes • Serves: 4

Ingredients

150 g (5¹/₂ oz) mixed pasta and noodles	*100 g (3¹/₂ oz) Roquefort cheese*
Salt and freshly ground black pepper	*150 g (5¹/₂ oz) full-cream plain yogurt*
1 red or yellow pepper	*5 ml (1 tsp) Worcestershire sauce*
100 g (3¹/₂ oz) bean sprouts	*150 g (5¹/₂ oz) Emmenthal cheese, grated or diced*
1 shallot, peeled and chopped	*15 ml (1 tbsp) finely chopped pistachio nuts*

Method

1

Cook the pasta in a large saucepan of lightly salted, boiling water, following the instructions on the packet, for 8-10 minutes or until al dente. Test the pasta several times during cooking to ensure it does not become overcooked.
Drain the pasta, rinse under cold running water, drain again and set aside to cool.

2

Slice the red or yellow pepper into quarters, remove and discard the stalk, core and seeds, then cut the flesh into dice. Rinse the bean sprouts in cold water and leave to drain. Set aside.

3

For the dressing, place the shallot in a blender or food processor with the Roquefort cheese and yogurt and blend to form a purée. Add salt and pepper to taste together with the Worcestershire sauce.

4

In a bowl, toss the pepper, bean sprouts, Emmenthal and pasta and noodles together, spoon onto 4 plates, then spoon the dressing over the salads. Sprinkle with pistachio nuts and serve.

Serving suggestion
Serve with fresh crusty bread or ciabatta.

Variations
Use mangetout or sugar-snap peas in place of bean sprouts. Use Gruyère cheese in place of Emmenthal.
Use walnuts or hazelnuts in place of the pistachio nuts.

Summer Pasta Salad

Lightly cooked summer vegetables are teamed with wholemeal pasta to create this delicious wholesome salad.

Preparation time: 40 minutes • Cooking time: 30 minutes • Serves 4

Ingredients

1 aubergine	*2 large tomatoes*
Salt and freshly ground black pepper	*60 ml (4 tbsp) olive oil*
1 courgette	*1 clove garlic, crushed*
1 red pepper	*225 g (8 oz) wholemeal pasta spirals*
1 green pepper	*15 ml (1 tbsp) vinegar*
1 onion	*2.5 ml (½ tsp) dry English mustard powder*

Method

1
Cut the aubergine into 1-cm (½-in) slices. Sprinkle the slices liberally with salt and allow to stand for 30 minutes.

2
Meanwhile, using a sharp knife, trim the courgette and cut into 5-mm (¼-in) slices. Set aside.

3
Cut the peppers in half and remove and discard the cores and seeds. Using a sharp knife, cut the pepper into thin strips. Peel and finely chop the onion. Set aside.

4
Cut a small cross in the skins of the tomatoes and plunge them into boiling water for 30 seconds. Remove the tomatoes and carefully peel away the skins. Cut the tomatoes into 8 and remove and discard the pips. Set aside.

5
Heat 30 ml (2 tbsp) of the olive oil in a frying pan and stir in the onion. Fry gently until transparent but not coloured.

6
Thoroughly rinse the salt from the aubergine slices and pat dry on absorbent kitchen paper. Roughly chop the slices.

7
Add the chopped aubergine, courgette, peppers, tomatoes and garlic to the cooked onion and fry very gently for 20 minutes, or until just soft, stirring occasionally. Season with salt and pepper, remove from the heat and set aside to cool.

8
Place the pasta spirals in a large saucepan and cover with boiling water. Sprinkle in a little salt and simmer for 10 minutes, or until al dente. Rinse the pasta in cold water and drain thoroughly.

9
Whisk together the remaining olive oil, vinegar and mustard in a small bowl. Season with salt and pepper.

10
Place the pasta and cooled vegetables in a serving dish and pour over the dressing, tossing the ingredients together to coat evenly. Serve well chilled.

Serving suggestion
Serve with fresh crusty French bread.

Variations
Use 2 leeks in place of the onion. Use wholegrain mustard in place of English mustard. Use chilli- or herb-flavoured oil in place of olive oil.

Cook's tip
Make sure that the aubergine is rinsed very thoroughly or the salad will be much too salty.

Courgette Salad

This healthy salad uses thinly sliced raw courgettes as a contrast in texture to the macaroni. Stuffed green olives add a touch of piquancy.

Preparation time: 15 minutes • Cooking time: 10 minutes • Serves: 4

Ingredients

225 g (8 oz) macaroni	*4-5 courgettes, thinly sliced*
Salt	*8 stuffed green olives, sliced*
4 tomatoes	*90 ml (6 tbsp) French dressing*

Method

1

Place the macaroni in a large saucepan and cover with boiling water. Add a little salt and simmer for 10 minutes, or until al dente. Rinse in cold water and drain well. Set aside.

2

Cut a small cross in the tops of each tomato and plunge into boiling water for 30 seconds. Remove from the water using a slotted spoon.

3

Carefully remove and discard the skins from the blanched tomatoes using a sharp knife. Chop the tomatoes coarsely.

4

Mix the macaroni, tomatoes, courgettes, olives and French dressing in a large bowl and chill in the refrigerator for 30 minutes before serving.

Serving suggestion

Serve with fresh wholemeal bread or hot garlic bread.

Variations

Use 450 g (1 lb) sliced mushrooms in place of courgettes. Use pitted black olives in place of green olives. Use lemon-flavoured mayonnaise in place of French dressing.

Cook's tip

If you prefer, the courgettes can be blanched in boiling water for 1 minute, then drained and cooled before mixing with the salad ingredients.

Spaghetti Salad Torcello

A tasty combination of pasta, tuna and ham, tossed together in a flavourful dressing.

Preparation time: 20 minutes, plus 30 minutes standing time • Cooking time: 8-12 minutes • Serves: 2-4

Ingredients

250 g (9 oz) spaghetti	*5 ml (1 tsp) anchovy paste*
15 ml (1 tbsp) vegetable oil	*15 ml (1 tbsp) lemon juice*
150 g (5½ oz) canned tuna	*5 ml (1 tsp) sugar*
200 g (7 oz) cooked ham	*Salt and freshly ground black pepper*
30 ml (2 tbsp) capers, drained	*125 ml (4 fl oz) olive oil*
1 egg yolk	*15 ml (2 tbsp) chopped fresh mixed herbs*

Method

1

Break the spaghetti into small pieces and place in a large saucepan of lightly salted, boiling water with the vegetable oil. Stir to mix.

2

Cook according to the instructions on the packet for 8-12 minutes, or until al dente, testing several times to ensure it does not overcook. When cooked, drain, rinse under cold running water, then drain again and set aside to cool.

3

Drain and flake the tuna and slice the ham into thin strips. Place the cooled spaghetti, tuna, ham and capers in a bowl and toss together to mix.

4

For the dressing, whisk the egg yolk, anchovy paste, lemon juice, sugar and salt and pepper to a thick paste in a bowl, then gradually whisk in the olive oil. Stir in the mixed herbs.

5

Spoon the dressing over the pasta mixture and toss together to mix well. Cover and set aside for 30 minutes before serving, to allow the flavours to mingle.

Serving suggestion
Serve with fresh bread or bread rolls.

Variations
Use chopped gherkins in place of capers. Use canned salmon in place of tuna.

Cook's tip
If using capers bottled in brine (salt water), rinse and drain thoroughly before use to remove as much brine as possible.

Mushroom Pasta Salad

Mushrooms are always delicious in a salad and this recipe, which combines them with wholemeal pasta shapes, is no exception.

Preparation time: 10 minutes, plus 1 hour marinating time • Cooking time: 10 minutes • Serves: 4

Ingredients

75 ml (5 tbsp) olive oil	*Salt and freshly ground black pepper*
Juice of 2 lemons	*225 g (8 oz) mushrooms*
5 ml (1 tsp) chopped fresh basil	*225 g (8 oz) wholemeal pasta shapes*
5 ml (1 tsp) chopped fresh parsley	*Fresh basil sprigs, to garnish*

Method

1
In a large bowl, mix together the olive oil, lemon juice, herbs and salt and pepper using a fork.

2
Thinly slice the mushrooms and add to the lemon dressing in the bowl, stirring well to coat the mushrooms evenly.

3
Cover the bowl with cling film and allow to sand in a cool place for at least 1 hour.

4
Place the pasta in a large saucepan and cover with boiling water. Season with a little salt and simmer for 10 minutes, or until just tender. Rinse the pasta in cold water and drain well.

5
Add the pasta to the marinated mushrooms and lemon dressing, mixing well to coat evenly.

6
Adjust the seasoning if necessary, then chill well before serving. Garnish with fresh basil sprigs.

Serving suggestion
Serve on a bed of mixed lettuce with crusty French bread.

Variations
Use a mixture of button and wild mushrooms. Use white or mixed pasta (i.e. tomato and spinach pasta) shapes in place of wholemeal pasta.

Pasta and Asparagus Salad

This elegant green salad is a wonderful way of making the most of fresh asparagus.

Preparation time: 15 minutes • Cooking time: 15 minutes • Serves: 4

Ingredients

115 g (4 oz) tagliatelle	*30 ml (2 tbsp) chopped fresh marjoram*
Salt and freshly ground black pepper	*1 lemon, peeled and segmented*
450 g (1 lb) asparagus, trimmed and cut into 2.5-cm (1-in) pieces	*Grated rind and juice of 1 lemon*
	90 ml (3 fl oz) olive oil
2 courgettes, cut into 5-cm (2-in) sticks	*A pinch of sugar (optional)*
	1 head of crisp lettuce
30 ml (2 tbsp) chopped fresh parsley	*1 head of endive or frisée lettuce*

Method

1

Place the pasta in a saucepan and cover with boiling water. Season with a little salt and simmer for 10-12 minutes, until just cooked or al dente.

2

Rinse the pasta under cold water, then set aside to cool completely. Cook the asparagus and courgettes in a saucepan of boiling water for 3-5 minutes, until just cooked and tender.

3

Drain the asparagus and courgettes into a colander and rinse them in cold water to refresh.

4

Place the pasta, cooked vegetables, herbs and lemon segments in a large bowl and mix them together carefully to avoid breaking up the vegetables.

5

In a separate bowl, mix together the lemon rind and juice, oil, sugar, if using, and salt and pepper.

6

Pour the lemon and oil dressing over the pasta mixture in the bowl and mix well to coat the vegetables and pasta evenly.

7

Arrange the lettuce and endive on serving plates and pile equal quantities of the asparagus and pasta mixture onto each plate. Serve.

Serving suggestion
Serve with thick slices of wholemeal bread.

Variations
Use mushrooms in place of asparagus. Use oranges in place of lemons. Use fettuccine or spaghetti in place of tagliatelle.

Cook's tip
Place the ingredients for the lemon dressing in a clean screw-top jar and shake vigorously to blend thoroughly.

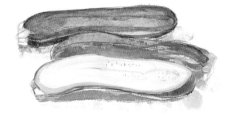

Cannelloni au Gratin

This classic baked pasta dish will always be a popular one with all the family.

Preparation time: 45 minutes • Cooking time: 30 minutes • Serves: 4

Ingredients

For the filling	For the tomato sauce
1 small onion	1 onion
1 clove garlic	1 clove garlic
15 ml (1 tbsp) vegetable oil	50-g (1³/4-oz) piece of streaky bacon
150 g (5¹/2 oz) frozen spinach, defrosted	15 ml (1 tbsp) olive oil
15 ml (1 tbsp) butter	15 ml (1 tbsp) plain flour
250 g (9 oz) minced beef	70 g (2¹/2 oz) tomato purée
30 ml (2 tbsp) grated Parmesan cheese	Chopped fresh basil
15 ml (1 tbsp) double cream	Chopped fresh marjoram
1 egg	Salt and freshly ground black pepper
Chopped fresh marjoram or dried oregano, to taste	375 ml (13 fl oz) meat stock
Salt and freshly ground black pepper, to taste	Grated Cheddar cheese, to sprinkle
250 g (9 oz) cannelloni	Flakes of butter, to dot surface

Method

1

For the filling, peel and chop the onion and garlic. Heat the vegetable oil in a pan, add the onion and garlic and cook until softened, stirring occasionally. Add the spinach and cook for 1-2 minutes, stirring. Remove the pan from the heat and transfer the spinach mixture to a bowl and set aside.

2

Melt the butter in the pan, add the minced beef and cook until browned all over. Add the meat to the spinach mixture with the Parmesan, cream and egg. Season with marjoram or oregano and salt and pepper, then mix all the ingredients together until well blended.

3

Spoon some of the filling into each cannelloni tube and set the filled cannelloni aside.

4

For the tomato sauce, peel and slice the onion and garlic and cut the bacon into small chunks. Heat the olive oil in a pan and cook the bacon for 5 minutes. Add the onion and garlic and cook until softened, stirring occasionally. Dust the bacon with the flour and allow to cook for 1 minute, stirring.

5

Stir in the tomato purée, then add basil, marjoram and salt and pepper to taste. Add the meat stock and bring to the boil. Reduce the heat and allow the sauce to simmer for about 10 minutes, stirring occasionally.

6

Pour a little of the sauce into the bottom of a greased shallow ovenproof dish. Arrange the filled cannelloni on top of the sauce, then cover with the remaining sauce.

7

Sprinkle with grated Cheddar cheese and dot with flakes of butter. Bake in a preheated oven at 180°C/350°F/Gas Mark 4 for about 30 minutes, until cooked and bubbling. Serve immediately.

Serving suggestions

Serve with a mixed leaf salad and fresh crusty bread, or fresh cooked vegetables such as green beans or baby corn cobs.

Variations

Use minced lamb, pork or chicken in place of beef. Use smoked bacon for the tomato sauce. Use 2-3 shallots in place of onion.

Courgette and Pine Nut Lasagne

This unusual vegetarian lasagne will leave your family or guests guessing as to the delicious ingredients used.

Preparation time: 35 minutes • Cooking time: 40 minutes • Serves: 4

Ingredients

12 sheets wholemeal lasagne	2.5 ml (½ tsp) grated nutmeg
85 g (3 oz) pine nuts	15 ml (1 tbsp) olive oil
25 g (1 oz) butter	1 large aubergine, sliced
675 g (1½ lb) courgettes, trimmed and sliced	10 ml (2 tsp) shoyu sauce (Japanese soy sauce)
280 g (10 0z) Ricotta cheese	85 g (3 oz) Cheddar cheese, grated
	Chopped fresh parsley, to garnish

Method

1

Place the lasagne in a large roasting tin and completely cover with boiling water. Leave for 10 minutes, then drain and set aside.

2

Place the pine nuts in a dry frying pan and roast gently for 2 minutes, stirring. Set aside.

3

Melt the butter in a frying pan, add the courgettes and a little water and cook until just tender.

4

Remove from the heat and combine the courgettes, pine nuts and Ricotta. Add nutmeg and mix well. Set aside.

5

In a separate pan, heat the olive oil, add the aubergine and cook for 4 minutes, stirring occasionally.

6

Add 150 ml (¼ pint) water and the shoyu sauce and simmer, covered, until the aubergine is soft, stirring occasionally.

7

Place the aubergine mixture in a blender or food processor and blend until smooth, adding a little extra water, if necessary, to make a sauce.

8

Place 4 strips of lasagne on the bottom of a greased 1.7-litre (3-pint) rectangular ovenproof dish and top with half the courgette mixture.

9

Place 4 more strips of lasagne over the courgettes and spread over half the aubergine sauce followed by the remainder of the courgettes.

10

Cover with the remaining lasagne and the remaining aubergine sauce.

11

Sprinkle the Cheddar cheese over the top and bake for about 40 minutes at 190°C/375°F/Gas Mark 5, until the cheese is melted and golden brown. Serve, garnished with chopped fresh parsley.

Serving suggestion

Serve with a crunchy mixed salad and baked potatoes.

Variations

Use chopped walnuts or almonds in place of pine nuts. Use lasagne verde for a change. Use mushrooms in place of courgettes.

Tagliatelle with Ham and Tomatoes

A fresh herb-flavoured baked pasta dish, served with a creamy sauce.

Preparation time: 20 minutes • Cooking time: 40 minutes • Serves: 4

ingredients

200 g (7 oz) green and plain tagliatelle	*60 ml (4 tbsp) milk*
Salt and freshly ground black pepper	*1 bunch of fresh chives*
750 g (1 lb 10 oz) beefsteak tomatoes, skinned	*½ bunch of fresh parsley*
250 g (9 oz) cooked ham	*400 g (14 oz) low-fat curd cheese*
3 eggs	*30 ml (2 tbsp) chopped fresh mixed herbs*
150 g (5½ oz) crème fraîche	*45-60 ml (3-4 tbsp) whipped cream*

Method

1
Cook the tagliatelle in a large saucepan of lightly salted, boiling water for 8-12 minutes, or according to the instructions on the packet, until cooked or al dente. Drain, rinse under boiling water, and drain again. Set aside and keep warm.

2
Meanwhile, cut the tomatoes into slices and cut the ham into small pieces. Set aside. Mix the eggs, crème fraîche and milk together and season to taste with salt and pepper. Set aside.

3
Wash and drain the chives and parsley, then finely chop. Grease a shallow ovenproof dish and cover with a layer of tomato slices. Sprinkle with salt and pepper and half the chopped herbs.

4
Arrange half the chopped ham on top, then make alternate layers with the pasta and the remaining tomatoes and ham, sprinkling with the remaining chives and parsley.

5
Cover with the egg and crème fraîche mixture and bake in a preheated oven at 200°C/400°F/Gas Mark 6 for 40 minutes, or until golden and bubbling.

6
Mix the curd cheese with the mixed herbs and whipped cream, and serve with the cooked pasta dish.

Serving suggestion
Serve with a mixed green salad and warm, fresh bread.

Variations
Use smoked ham in place of unsmoked ham. Use spaghetti or fettuccine in place of tagliatelle.

Oven-Baked Spaghetti

A trouble-free, popular dish – ideal for a midweek family meal.

Preparation time: 15 minutes • Cooking time: 30 minutes • Serves: 4

Ingredients

225 g (8 oz) cooked wholemeal spaghetti	*5 ml (1 tsp) dried oregano*
2 x 400-g (14-oz) cans tomatoes, roughly chopped	*Salt and freshly ground black pepper*
	115 g (4 oz) Cheddar cheese
1 large onion, grated	*30 ml (2 tbsp) Parmesan cheese, grated*

Method

1
Grease 4 individual ovenproof dishes and place a quarter of the spaghetti in each.

2
Spoon the tomatoes over the top.

3
Add the onion, sprinkle with oregano and season well with salt and pepper. Stir to mix.

4
Thinly slice the Cheddar cheese and arrange over the top of the spaghetti mixture.

5
Sprinkle with Parmesan cheese and bake at 180°C/350°F/Gas Mark 4 for 25-30 minutes, until golden brown and bubbling. Serve hot.

Serving suggestion
Serve with hot garlic or herb bread.

Variations
Use white spaghetti in place of wholemeal. Use Red Leicester cheese in place of Cheddar.

Cook's tip
This dish can be cooked in 1 large casserole if required, but add about 10 minutes to the cooking time.

Ratatouille Lasagne

An appetising Mediterranean vegetable lasagne – a satisfying choice for lunch or supper.

Preparation time: 30 minutes • Cooking time: 35 minutes • Serves: 4-6

Ingredients

6 sheets lasagne verde or wholemeal lasagne	30-45 ml (2-3 tbsp) tomato purée
30-45 ml (2-3 tbsp) olive oil	A little vegetable stock
2 onions, finely chopped	Salt and freshly ground black pepper
2 cloves garlic, crushed	**For the white sauce**
2 large aubergines, chopped	25 g (1 oz) butter
1 courgette, thinly sliced	25 g (1 oz) plain wholemeal flour
1 green pepper, seeded and chopped	300 ml (½ pint) milk
1 red pepper, seeded and chopped	40 g (1½ oz) Parmesan cheese, grated
400-g (14-oz) can chopped tomatoes	Fresh parsley sprigs, to garnish

Method

1

Cook the lasagne in boiling, salted water for 12-15 minutes. Plunge into a bowl of cold water to prevent overcooking or sticking.

2

Heat the oil in a frying pan and fry the onion and garlic until soft.

3

Add the aubergine, courgette and peppers and cook until soft, stirring occasionally.

4

Add the tomatoes with their juice and the tomato purée and simmer until tender, stirring occasionally. It may be necessary to add a little stock at this stage. Season well and set aside.

5

Make the white sauce by melting the butter in a small saucepan. Add the flour and cook for 1 minute, stirring.

6

Add the milk slowly, stirring constantly, bring to the boil and simmer for about 3 minutes. Remove from the heat.

7

Grease a deep ovenproof dish. Layer the ratatouille and lasagne strips, starting with the ratatouille and finishing with a layer of lasagne.

8

Pour over the white sauce and sprinkle the Parmesan cheese over the top.

9

Bake in a preheated oven at 180°C/350°F/Gas Mark 4 for about 35 minutes, until golden brown and bubbling. Garnish with parsley sprigs before serving. Serve hot.

Serving suggestion

Serve with crusty bread rolls and a green salad.

Variations

If aubergine is not available, use 225 g (8 oz) sliced mushrooms instead. Use 450 g (1 lb) fresh tomatoes, skinned and chopped, in place of canned tomatoes. Use 3-4 leeks in place of onions.

Spaghetti with Roquefort

Roquefort has a delightful creamy-rich texture with a pungent, slightly salty flavour – qualities which make it the ideal basis for a luxury pasta sauce.

Preparation time: 15 minutes • Cooking time: 8-12 minutes • Serves: 4

Ingredients

500 g (1 lb 2 oz) spaghetti	125 ml (4 fl oz) whipped cream
Salt and freshly ground black pepper	30 ml (2 tbsp) shelled toasted sunflower seeds
200 g (7 oz) Roquefort cheese	Fresh herbs, to garnish

Method

1

Cook the spaghetti in a large saucepan of lightly salted, boiling water for 8-12 minutes, or until just cooked or al dente. Drain well and keep warm.

2

Mix the Roquefort cheese to a purée with the whipped cream and season with pepper to taste.

3

Toss the Roquefort cheese with the spaghetti, mixing well. Set aside for 1 minute for the sauce to be absorbed, then spoon onto warmed serving plates.

4

Sprinkle the sunflower seeds over the spaghetti sauce and serve immediately, garnished with fresh herbs.

Serving suggestions

Serve with a mixed leaf salad or fresh cooked vegetables, such as broccoli and carrots.

Variations

Use Stilton in place of Roquefort. Use tagliatelle or fettuccine in place of spaghetti. Use pumpkin or sesame seeds in place of sunflower seeds.

Tortellini with Parma Ham and Cream

Ready-prepared cheese-filled tortellini are combined with Parma Ham, a fresh sage-flavoured tomato sauce and fennel, and baked with a creamy topping.

Preparation time: 20 minutes • Cooking time: 50 minutes • Serves: 4

Ingredients

250 g (9 oz) fresh cheese-filled tortellini	1 small bulb of fennel, weighing about 200 g (7 oz)
45 ml (3 tbsp) olive oil	
6 spring onions, cut into rings	2 eggs
1 clove garlic, crushed	200 ml (7 fl oz) double cream
250 g (9 oz) tomatoes, skinned and sliced	150 g (5½ oz) soured cream
150 g (5½ oz) Parma ham, cut into strips	25 g (1 oz) mature Gouda cheese, grated
Chopped fresh sage	25 g (1 oz) butter
Salt and freshly ground pepper	Fresh sage sprigs, to garnish

Method

1

Cook the tortellini in a large pan of boiling, salted water, turning frequently, until just tender or al dente. Drain and set aside.

2

Heat the olive oil in a frying pan over a medium heat, add the spring onions and cook for about 3 minutes, stirring frequently, until softened.

3

Add the garlic and cook for 2 minutes, stirring. Stir in the tomatoes, Parma ham and sage to taste, season with salt and pepper and set aside.

4

Cut the fennel bulb in half and trim away the green tops. Slice the bulb and cook in a pan of boiling water for about 5 minutes. Drain and set aside.

5

Place the cooked tortellini in the bottom of a greased ovenproof dish. Spread over the tomato and Parma ham mixture and top with the cooked fennel.

6

In a bowl, beat the eggs with the cream and soured cream and season with salt and pepper. Pour over the pasta and vegetables in the dish and sprinkle the cheese on top. Dot with flakes of butter.

7

Bake in a preheated oven at 180°C/350°F/Gas Mark 4 for about 30 minutes, until golden and bubbling. Serve immediately, garnished with sage sprigs.

Serving suggestion

Serve with a green leaf and fresh herb salad, tossed in garlic-flavoured olive oil.

Variations

Use pastrami or thinly sliced salami in place of Parma ham. Use Mozzarella cheese in place of Gouda.

Tagliatelle Verde alla Ricotta

In this traditional Italian dish, green tagliatelle is baked with a creamy Ricotta cheese sauce flavoured with nutmeg.

Preparation time: 20 minutes • Cooking time: 30 minutes • Serves: 4

Ingredients

500 g (1 lb 2 oz) tagliatelle verde	*Ground nutmeg*
Salt	*50 g (1¾ oz) grated Parmesan cheese*
500 g (1 lb 2 oz) Ricotta or low-fat curd cheese	*70 g (2½ oz) butter flakes*

Method

1

Cook the tagliatelle in a large saucepan of lightly salted, boiling water for 8-12 minutes, or until al dente. Drain well.

2

Place the Ricotta or low-fat curd cheese in a bowl and stir in 30 ml (2 tbsp) boiling water together with the nutmeg and salt to taste, to form a creamy consistency.

3

Grease an ovenproof dish and arrange the tagliatelle and cheese sauce in alternate layers, finishing with a layer of the cheese mixture. Sprinkle with the Parmesan cheese and butter flakes.

4

Bake in a preheated oven at 180°C/350°F/Gas Mark 4 for about 30 minutes, until golden brown. Serve hot.

Serving suggestion

Serve with a tomato, pepper and onion salad.

Variations

Use fettuccine or pasta shapes in place of tagliatelle. Use Cheddar cheese in place of Parmesan.

Cook's tip

For the best flavour, freshly grate a whole nutmeg using a special nutmeg grater or a very fine grater.

Pasta with Blue Cheese

In this special-occasion dish, freshly made pasta noodles are tossed with a creamy sauce flavoured
with blue cheese and diced dried apricots.

Preparation time: 1 hour, plus 2 hours drying time • Cooking time: 15 minutes • Serves: 6

Ingredients

500 g (1 1b 2 oz) plain flour	*115 g (4 oz) ready-to-eat dried apricots*
Salt and freshly ground black pepper	*300 ml (½ pint) double cream*
5 eggs	*50 ml (2 fl oz) milk*
15 ml (1 tbsp) olive oil	*2 egg yolks*
115 g (4 oz) blue cheese, such as Roquefort or Stilton	*55 g (2 oz) pine nuts*
	½ bunch of fresh chives

Method

1

In a bowl, mix together the flour, a pinch of salt and eggs to form a soft ball of dough.

2

Quarter and flatten each piece of dough and dredge with plenty of flour. Flour the rollers of a pasta machine
or a rolling pin and either pass the dough through the machine or roll out.

3

Continue rolling the pasta until thin. Flour frequently during the process. Thread the dough strips through a tagliatelle cutter,
or cut into strips with a knife. Dredge the noodles with flour and set aside to dry for 2 hours.

4

Bring a saucepan of salted water to the boil with the oil. Cook the pasta for 2-4 minutes, stirring with a fork, or until al dente.
Drain the tagliatelle and rinse in plenty of cold water to prevent sticking. Set aside.

5

Crumble the blue cheese and push through a sieve with the back of a spoon. Set aside. Cut the apricots into strips,
then dice and set aside.

6

Slowly heat the cream in a saucepan. Stir in the blue cheese and milk, then blend until smooth with
a hand-held electric mixer or whisk.

7

While the sauce is hot, stir in the tagliatelle and apricots and season to taste as necessary.
Heat through quickly so that the sauce does not curdle.

8

Toss the pasta with the sauce using two forks. Remove from the heat and stir in the egg yolks and pine nuts, mixing well.

9

Chop the chives finely and sprinkle over the tagliatelle. Serve immediately.

Serving suggestion

Serve with a green side salad and crusty bread rolls.

Variations

Use ready-to-eat dried peaches or pears in place of apricots. Use chopped almonds or cashew nuts in place of pine nuts.

Spaghetti with Tuna and Mussel Sauce

A quick-and-easy fish and seafood sauce for a delicious after-work treat.

Preparation time: 15 minutes • Cooking time: 25 minutes • Serves: 4

Ingredients

250 g (9 oz) tomatoes	Salt and freshly ground black pepper
200-g (7-oz) can mussels	30-45 ml (2-3 tbsp) finely chopped fresh parsley
375 g (13 oz) canned tuna	
4 cloves garlic	400 g (14 oz) spaghetti
30 ml (2 tbsp) olive oil	15 ml (1 tbsp) sunflower oil

Method

1

Immerse the tomatoes in boiling water for 30 seconds, then plunge into cold water.
Remove and discard the skins and chop the flesh into chunks. Set aside.

2

Drain the mussels and tuna, and flake the tuna with a fork. Peel and finely chop the garlic. Set aside.

3

Heat the olive oil in a pan, add the garlic and cook until softened, stirring.

4

Add the tomato chunks and cook for 5 minutes, then add the mussels, tuna and a little liquid from the canned mussels.
Mix well and cook for 5 minutes until heated through, stirring occasionally.

5

Season to taste with salt and pepper, then stir in the parsley. Keep warm.

6

Meanwhile, bring a large saucepan of lightly salted water to the boil and add the spaghetti with the sunflower oil.
Simmer for 8-10 minutes, stirring occasionally with a fork, until just cooked or al dente.

7

Rinse and drain the spaghetti and serve with the fish sauce spooned over the top.

Serving suggestion
Serve with a shredded mixed vegetable salad.

Variations
Use fresh basil or chives in place of parsley. Use canned salmon in place of tuna. Use cooked, shelled prawns in place of mussels.

Cook's tip
Choose tuna canned in water rather than in brine to keep sodium content down.

Salmon and Fennel Lasagne

Thin strips of pasta are precooked and then layered with salmon and béchamel sauce. Fish stock is poured over and the dish is then topped with cheese and cooked in the oven. Absolutely mouthwatering!

Preparation time: 40 minutes, plus 30 minutes standing time • Cooking time: 30 minutes • Serves: 4

Ingredients

350 g (12 oz) plain flour, sifted	**For the béchamel sauce**
Salt and freshly ground black pepper	300 ml (½ pint) milk
	½ small onion, roughly chopped
3 eggs, beaten	A blade of mace
600 g (1 lb 5 oz) skinless salmon (in one long strip if possible)	A few fresh parsley stalks
	5 white or green peppercorns
5 ml (1 tsp) fennel seeds	1 bay leaf
250 ml (9 fl oz) fish stock	25 g (1 oz) butter
25 g (1 oz) butter	20 g (¾ oz) flour
60 ml (4 tbsp) grated Cheddar cheese	Salt and freshly ground white pepper

Method

1

To make the pasta dough, mix together the flour, a good pinch of salt and the eggs in a bowl. Set aside to rest for 30 minutes, then roll out very thinly into long lasagne strips.

2

Partly cook the pasta in a saucepan of salted boiling water for 1 minute. Drain, then lay out on damp tea-towels without overlapping the strips.

3

Meanwhile, cut the salmon into thin slices. Remove and discard all the bones and set aside.

4

To make the béchamel sauce, place the milk, onion, mace, parsley stalks, peppercorns and bay leaf in a saucepan and slowly bring to a simmer. Lower the temperature and leave for about 10 minutes.

5

Melt the butter in a saucepan over a medium heat, stir in the flour and cook, stirring continuously, for 1 minute. Remove from the heat and strain in the flavoured milk.

6

Gradually heat the sauce, stirring or whisking continuously, until boiling. Reduce the heat and simmer, stirring, for 3 minutes. Season with salt and pepper.

7

Grease an ovenproof dish and arrange the lasagne over the base. Add a layer of béchamel sauce, then a few fennel seeds, salmon and salt and pepper followed by another layer of lasagne. Continue layering the ingredients until used up, finishing with a layer of pasta.

8

Pour over the fish stock, dot with butter, then sprinkle over the cheese. Cook in a preheated oven at 200°C/400°F/Gas Mark 6 for about 30 minutes, or until the fish stock has been almost completely absorbed and the top is slightly crisp and golden brown. Serve hot.

Serving suggestion

Serve with slices of wholemeal or soda bread and a crisp leaf salad.

Variations

Use cumin or sesame seeds in place of the fennel seeds, for a different flavour.

Pasta with Leeks and Mussels

This pasta dish is relatively quick and easy to prepare. Spiral-shaped pasta is tossed with cooked mussels and sautéed leeks and a sauce of the reduced cooking juices. The thinly sliced ham adds flavour and also makes an attractive garnish.

Preparation time: 25 minutes • Cooking time: 30 minutes • Serves: 6

Ingredients

1.7 litres (3 pints) fresh mussels in their shells	450 g (1 lb) fresh pasta spirals
1 shallot, chopped	15 ml (1 tbsp) olive oil
125 ml (4 fl oz) white wine	15 g (½ oz) butter
2 medium leeks	2 slices ham, chopped or thinly sliced
75 ml (6 fl oz) double cream	Chopped fresh chives, to garnish
Salt and freshly ground black pepper	

Method

1
Scrub the mussels, remove the beards and wash in several changes of water.

2
Place the mussels and shallot in a large saucepan and add the wine. Cover and cook over high heat for about 5 minutes.

3
Allow to cool, then remove the opened mussels from their shells. Discard any mussels that remain unopened. Reserve the cooking liquid and set aside.

4
Quarter each leek lengthways, wash thoroughly and drain. Thinly slice each quarter. Place the leeks, cream and salt and pepper in a saucepan, cover and cook over a low heat for 10 minutes, stirring occasionally. Set aside.

5
Meanwhile, in a large saucepan of boiling water, cook the pasta with the olive oil for 5-6 minutes, stirring the pasta as it cooks to prevent sticking. Drain, rinse in cold water, then drain again. Set aside.

6
Strain the mussel cooking liquid through a sieve lined with muslin. Measure out about 125 ml (4 fl oz).

7
Add the shelled mussels and the mussel liquid to the leek and cream mixture and cook for 4 minutes, stirring continuously.

8
Melt the butter in a deep frying pan, add the pasta and ham and reheat gently, stirring. Season to taste with salt and pepper.

9
When the pasta is heated through, add the cream, leek and mussel sauce, toss to mix and serve immediately, garnished with the chopped chives.

Serving suggestion
Serve with a mixed dark leaf salad.

Variations
Use 2 onions in place of leeks. Use smoked ham for a change.

Pasta with Cockles

This seafood pasta sauce is enriched and flavoured with white wine, garlic and butter.

Preparation time: 10 minutes • Cooking time: 20 minutes • Serves: 4

Ingredients

450 g (1 1b) fresh cockles in their shells	*Salt and freshly ground black pepper*
125 ml (4 fl oz) white wine	*55 g (2 oz) butter*
1 shallot, chopped	*1 clove garlic, chopped*
300 g (10½ oz) fresh pasta	*15 ml (1 tbsp) chopped fresh parsley*

Method

1
Place the cockles in a large saucepan, pour in the wine, add the shallot and cook over a high heat. Shake the saucepan frequently until the cockles open. Remove from the heat and set the pan aside until the cockles are cool enough to handle.

2
Remove the cockles from their shells and set aside. Discard the shells, cooking water and shallot.

3
Cook the pasta in a large saucepan of lightly salted, boiling water for about 4 minutes, or until al dente. Rinse in hot water and set aside to drain.

4
Melt the butter in a saucepan, add the garlic, chopped parsley, pasta and the cockles. Season with salt and pepper.

5
Heat gently, stirring continuously, until the pasta is heated through. Serve immediately.

Serving suggestions
Serve with thick slices of fresh crusty bread or fresh cooked vegetables, such as shredded cabbage and courgettes.

Variations
Use other shellfish, such as whelks or clams, in place of cockles. Use wholemeal pasta in place of white pasta.

Cook's tip
When the cockles are cooked and cooled you can remove them from their shells, but keep them in the cooking juice until needed, to prevent them from drying out.

Rock Salmon in Paprika Sauce

Rock salmon is a firm, succulent fish – ideal for use in kebabs or fish casseroles. In this recipe, it is perfectly complemented by a creamy paprika-flavoured sauce and ribbon pasta.

Preparation time: 20 minutes • Cooking time: 15-20 minutes • Serves: 4

Ingredients

450 g (1 1b) rock salmon fillets	1 clove garlic, crushed
Lemon juice	25 g (1 oz) plain flour
1 bay leaf	300 ml (½ pint) milk
A slice of onion	15 ml (1 tbsp) chopped fresh parsley
6 red or green peppercorns	5 ml (1 tsp) chopped fresh thyme
25 g (1 oz) butter	5 ml (1 tsp) tomato purée
55 g (2 oz) button mushrooms, sliced	Salt and freshly ground black pepper
1 small red pepper, seeded and sliced	25 g (8 oz) fresh pasta, cooked
1 shallot, finely chopped	30 ml (2 tbsp) soured cream or plain yogurt
10 ml (2 tsp) paprika	

Method

1

Cut the rock salmon into 2.5-cm (1-in) chunks. Place in an ovenproof dish with a generous squeeze of lemon juice, bay leaf, onion, peppercorns and just enough water to cover. Cover with a lid and poach the fish for about 10 minutes in a preheated oven at 180°C/350°F/Gas Mark 4.

2

Meanwhile, melt the butter in a saucepan and stir in the mushrooms, pepper, shallot, paprika and garlic. Cook gently until the pepper begins to soften, stirring occasionally.

3

Stir the flour into the mushroom and pepper mixture. Gradually add the milk, stirring until the sauce has thickened.

4

Remove the fish from the dish and strain off and reserve the cooking liquid. Stir enough of the liquid into the pepper sauce to make it of a coating consistency. Add the parsley, thyme and tomato purée to the sauce and simmer for 2-3 minutes, stirring. Season to taste with salt and pepper.

5

Arrange the hot, cooked pasta on a serving plate and place the rock salmon on top. Coat with the paprika sauce and spoon over the soured cream or yogurt to serve. Serve immediately.

Serving suggestion

Serve with a mixed leaf salad.

Variations

Use any other firm-fleshed white fish, such as monkfish, in place of the rock salmon. Use courgettes in place of mushrooms. Use crème fraîche in place of soured cream.

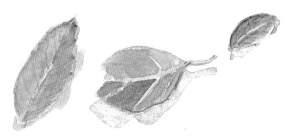

Spaghetti Carbonara

This classic pasta dish is always a firm favourite, with its winning combination of bacon,
cream and Parmesan cheese.

Preparation time: 15 minutes • Cooking time: 15-20 minutes • Serves: 4

Ingredients

400 g (14 oz) spaghetti verde	100 g (3½ oz) fresh Parmesan cheese
Salt	6 eggs
15 ml (1 tbsp) olive oil	30-45 ml (2-3 tbsp) double cream
250 g (9 oz) streaky bacon	Coarsely ground black pepper
15 g (½ oz) butter	Freshly grated nutmeg

Method

1

Bring a large saucepan of lightly salted water to the boil and add the spaghetti and the olive oil. Cook for 8-10 minutes,
or until al dente, stirring the spaghetti occasionally with a fork. Drain well and keep warm.

2

Cut the bacon into small pieces. Melt the butter in a large frying pan, add the bacon and fry for about 5 minutes,
until cooked, stirring frequently.

3

Grate the Parmesan cheese into a bowl and mix with the eggs and cream. Season with pepper and nutmeg and set aside.

4

Add the spaghetti to the bacon, then carefully pour the egg and cream mixture over the pasta and mix thoroughly.
Remove the pan from the heat. Serve immediately with plenty of freshly ground pepper.

Serving suggestion

Serve with a rocket and frisée salad.

Variations

Use smoked bacon for extra flavour. Use white or wholemeal spaghetti in place of green spaghetti.
Use mature Cheddar or Gruyère cheese in place of Parmesan.

Chinese-Style Noodles

This unusual noodle-based dish contains pork, prawns and mixed vegetables, for an exciting flavour experience.

Preparation time: 20 minutes, plus 1 hour marinating time • Cooking time: 30 minutes • Serves: 4

Ingredients

400 g (14 oz) lean pork	150 g (5½ oz) fresh spinach leaves
90 ml (6 tbsp) soy sauce	3 small leeks
2.5 ml (½ tsp) sugar	300 g (10½ oz) thin Chinese noodles
15 ml (1 tbsp) cornflour	15 ml (1 tbsp) olive oil
4 eggs	200-g (7-oz) can bamboo shoots, drained
Salt and freshly ground black pepper	200 g (7 oz) cooked, shelled prawns
105 ml (7 tbsp) soya oil	

Method

1

Slice the pork into thin strips and place in a shallow, non-metallic dish. Mix the soy sauce with the sugar and cornflour and pour over the meat. Stir to mix well, cover and set aside in a cool place to marinate for 1 hour.

2

In a bowl, beat the eggs and add salt to taste. Heat 30 ml (2 tbsp) of the soya oil in a frying pan, add the eggs and cook gently until cooked and lightly set. Remove the pan from the heat, set aside to cool, then slice into strips. Set aside.

3

Wash the spinach, drain, then slice into strips. Wash the leeks and thinly slice into rings. Set aside.

4

Heat a further 30 ml (2 tbsp) soya oil in a pan. Lift the pork out of the marinade using a slotted spoon and add to the pan. Stir-fry the pork for about 2 minutes, then add the marinade and stir-fry for a further 3-4 minutes, or until cooked and tender. Remove from the pan, place on a plate and keep warm.

5

Cook the Chinese noodles as directed on the packet in a large saucepan of boiling, salted water with the olive oil. Test the noodles to ensure that they do not overcook. Drain well and set aside. Keep warm.

6

Heat the remaining soya oil with the cooking juices in the pan in which the pork was cooked, add the spinach, leeks and bamboo shoots and stir-fry for 2-3 minutes over a high heat. Add the pork and strips of cooked egg. Add the prawns and season to taste with salt and pepper. Mix in the noodles and reheat briefly before serving hot.

Serving suggestion

Serve with a crisp green salad and prawn crackers.

Variations

Use green cabbage, finely shredded, in place of spinach. Use lean lamb or beef in place of pork.
Use cooked, shelled mussels in place of prawns.

Meat Ravioli with Red Pepper Sauce

Red-tinged, pepper-flavoured pasta dough is thinly rolled, cut into squares, filled with a delicious meat stuffing and served with a creamy red pepper sauce.

Preparation time: 30 minutes, plus 1 hour standing time • Cooking time: 15 minutes • Serves: 4

Ingredients

2 large red peppers, seeded	15 ml (1 tbsp) finely chopped fresh parsley
200 g (7 oz) plain flour, sifted	½ onion, chopped
Salt and freshly ground black pepper	125 ml (4 fl oz) single cream
2 eggs	85 g (3 oz) butter
200 g (7 oz) cooked minced beef	

Method

1

Place the red peppers in a food processor with 60 ml (4 tbsp) water and blend until smooth. Place in a small bowl and set aside allowing time for the pulp to rise to the surface. This takes approximately 30 minutes.

2

To make the pasta dough, place the flour in a bowl with a pinch of salt. Add 1 egg and 45 ml (3 tbsp) of the pepper pulp (not the juice).

3

Mix together thoroughly and form into a ball. Set the dough aside for 30 minutes.

4

In a separate bowl, mix together the minced beef, parsley and onion and season with salt and pepper. Set aside.

5

Roll the dough out very thinly using a pasta machine if available, or a rolling pin. Cut into small squares. Place a little of the filling on half of the cut squares. Beat the remaining egg and brush the edges of the squares with the egg. Cover with another square of dough and seal the edges by pinching together with your fingers.

6

Bring a large saucepan of salted water to the boil and cook the ravioli for about 3 minutes – longer if you prefer your pasta well cooked.

7

While the ravioli are cooking, prepare the pepper sauce. Heat the cream with 125 ml (4 fl oz) of the red pepper pulp. Bring to the boil, then whisk in the butter.

8

Drain the ravioli, then pat dry with a clean tea-towel. Serve immediately with the hot cream-pepper sauce.

Serving suggestion

Serve with a mixed dark leaf salad and garlic bread.

Variations

Add a little wine vinegar (5 ml/1 tsp) and a few drops of Tabasco to the sauce to give it a slightly peppery taste. Use cooked minced lamb or pork in place of beef. Use fresh coriander in place of parsley.

Cook's tip

When rolling out the dough, flour it well so that it does not stick to the pasta machine rollers or rolling pin.

Siennese Macaroni

A sophisticated yet easy-to-make dish of macaroni in a creamy cheese sauce with ham and walnuts, flavoured with fresh basil.

Preparation time: 15 minutes • Cooking time: 25 minutes • Serves: 4

Ingredients

500 g (1 1b 2 oz) macaroni	100 g (3½ oz) cooked lean ham
Salt and freshly ground black pepper	250 ml (9 fl oz) double cream
A small handful of fresh basil leaves	85 g (3 oz) grated fresh Parmesan cheese
125 g (4½ oz) shelled walnuts	Fresh basil sprigs, to garnish
50 g (1¾ oz) butter	

Method

1
Cook the macaroni in a large saucepan of lightly salted, boiling water for 8-12 minutes, or until al dente.
Drain well and keep warm.

2
Shred the basil leaves and finely chop the walnuts. Set aside. Melt the butter in a saucepan, add the basil and walnuts and cook gently for about 10 minutes, stirring occasionally.

3
Finely chop the ham and add it to the pan with the cream. Season to taste with salt and pepper.

4
Add the macaroni and stir over a low heat so that the sauce flows into the hollows of the macaroni.

5
Stir in half of the Parmesan, then serve immediately on warmed serving plates, sprinkled with the remaining Parmesan.
Garnish with fresh basil sprigs.

Serving suggestion
Serve with thick slices of fresh wholemeal or ciabatta bread.

Variations
Use parsley or chives in place of basil. Use pecan nuts or cashew nuts in place of walnuts.
Use cooked chicken or turkey in place of ham.

Pasta Soufflé

A soufflé with a difference, made using pasta, to create an appealing supper or lunch dish.

Preparation time: 30 minutes • Cooking time: 35 minutes • Serves: 4

Ingredients

250 g (9 oz) tagliatelle	500 g (1 lb 2 oz) mixed minced pork and beef
Salt and freshly ground black pepper	Ground paprika
2 medium onions	Chopped fresh thyme
1 clove garlic	500 g (1 lb 2 oz) tomatoes, skinned and chopped or sliced
40 g (1½ oz) butter	100 g (3½ oz) Cheddar cheese, grated

Method

1

Cook the pasta in a large saucepan of lightly salted, boiling water for about 8 minutes, or until al dente, stirring occasionally. Drain well and keep warm.

2

Meanwhile, peel the onions and garlic and thinly slice. Melt the butter in a pan and cook the onion and garlic until softened.

3

Add the minced pork and beef and cook until browned all over, stirring frequently. Season to taste with salt and pepper, paprika and thyme.

4

Add the tomatoes to the pan and simmer for about 5 minutes, stirring occasionally.

5

Place about two-thirds of the pasta in a greased ovenproof dish, cover with the meat mixture, then top with the remaining pasta.

6

Sprinkle with grated cheese and bake in a preheated oven at 220°C/425°F/Gas Mark 7 for about 35 minutes, until golden brown and bubbling. Serve hot.

Serving suggestions

Serve with a chopped mixed green salad or fresh cooked vegetables, such as cauliflower and baby carrots.

Variations

Use chicken and ham or lamb and pork in place of pork and beef. Use 2 leeks in place of onions.
Use Parmesan cheese in place of Cheddar cheese.

Lasagne Rolls

In this unusual dish, rolled up sheets of lasagne enclose a delicious creamy chicken and mushroom filling.

Preparation time: 15 minutes • Cooking time: 25 minutes • Serves: 4

Ingredients

Salt and freshly ground black pepper	*225 g (8 oz) boned chicken breast, cut into thin strips*
10 ml (2 tsp) vegetable oil	
8 sheets of lasagne	*25 g (1 oz) plain flour*
25 g (1 oz) butter	*150 ml (¼ pint) milk*
55 g (2 oz) button mushrooms, sliced	*115 g (4 oz) Gruyère or Cheddar cheese, grated*

Method

1
Fill a large saucepan two-thirds full with salted water. Add the oil and bring to the boil.

2
Add 1 sheet of lasagne, wait for about 2 minutes, then add another sheet. Cook only a few lasagne sheets at a time. After about 6-7 minutes, or when tender, remove from the boiling water and rinse under cold water. Allow to drain. Repeat this process until all the lasagne is cooked. Set aside.

3
Melt half the butter in a small frying pan, add the mushrooms and the chicken and cook for about 5 minutes, until the chicken is cooked and tender, stirring frequently. Set aside.

4
In a small saucepan, melt the remaining butter. Stir in the flour and cook for 1 minute.

5
Remove the pan from the heat and gradually add the milk, stirring well and returning the pan to the heat between additions, to thicken the sauce.

6
Beat the sauce well and cook for 3 minutes, until it is thick and smooth, stirring.

7
Pour the sauce into the frying pan with the chicken and the mushrooms. Add half the cheese and mix well. Season to taste with salt and pepper.

8
Lay the sheets of lasagne on a clean work surface and divide the chicken mixture equally between them.

9
Spread the chicken mixture evenly over each lasagne sheet and roll up lengthways, like a Swiss roll.

10
Place the rolls in an ovenproof dish. Sprinkle with the remaining cheese and grill under a preheated grill until the cheese is bubbling and golden brown. Serve hot.

Serving suggestion
Serve piping hot with a fresh green salad and crusty French bread.

Variations
For a delicious vegetarian alternative, use Stilton cheese and 115 g (4 oz) broccoli florets instead of the chicken breasts. Use turkey in place of chicken. Use courgettes in place of mushrooms.

Cook's tip
Precooked lasagne is widely available at most supermarkets and does not require as much initial cooking. If available, try preparing this dish with sheets of fresh lasagne, which require the least precooking of all.

Rabbit Ravioli with Tarragon

This is a relatively time-consuming, unusual pasta dish to prepare, but well worth the effort.

Preparation time: 1 hour • Cooking time: 1 hour 50 minutes • Serves: 6

Ingredients

350 g (12 oz) plain flour	*5 sprigs of fresh tarragon*
Salt and freshly ground black pepper	*½ leek, finely chopped*
	1 onion, finely chopped
4 eggs, beaten	*1 carrot, finely chopped*
30 ml (2 tbsp) olive oil	*1 bouquet garni (parsley, thyme, bay leaf)*
3 rabbit thighs	*50 ml (2 fl oz) double cream*

Method

1

Place the flour in a bowl with 5 ml (1 tsp) salt. Add 3 eggs. Mix with your fingers to make a dough and form into a ball. Set aside to rest.

2

Heat the oil in a pan, add the rabbit and fry until lightly coloured, stirring occasionally.

3

Remove the tarragon leaves from 3 sprigs, reserve the stalks for the stock and chop the leaves.

4

Add the leek, onion, carrot, tarragon stalks and bouquet garni to the rabbit. Cook for 2 minutes. Add 850 ml (1½ pints) water. Bring to the boil, cover and cook over a low heat for 1 hour 30 minutes, stirring occasionally.

5

When cooked, remove the rabbit meat and discard the bones. Mince the meat. Mix the minced meat with ¾ of the tarragon leaves. Season with salt and pepper and set aside. Strain the stock through a fine sieve and set aside.

6

Divide the dough into smaller, flat rounds, and thread these through a pasta machine to form into thin pasta strips.

7

Cut the pasta into rectangles. Mix 30 ml (2 tbsp) stock into the minced meat mixture and place about a teaspoon of the mixture in the centre of each triangle.

8

Brush the edges of the rectangles with the remaining beaten egg and fold over one side. Pinch the edges together with your fingers. Shape into rounds using a pastry cutter and set aside.

9

Cook the ravioli for 5 minutes in a large saucepan of salted boiling water with 1 sprig of tarragon. Remove with a slotted spoon, drain, then place on a damp tea-towel. Keep hot.

10

Meanwhile, reduce 300 ml (½ pint) of the rabbit stock by half by boiling it rapidly, uncovered, in a saucepan. Add the cream and remaining chopped tarragon. Heat through gently and season.

11

Serve the ravioli and cream soup in soup plates. Garnish with the remaining tarragon sprigs, left whole or chopped. Serve immediately.

Serving suggestion

Serve with fresh cooked vegetables, such as broccoli and baby corn cobs.

Variations

Use chicken in place of rabbit. Use coriander in place of tarragon.

Spaghetti Bolognese

This is probably the most well-known and popular pasta dish of all. In this version, the meat sauce is enriched by red wine and flavoured with thyme and basil.

Preparation time: 20 minutes • Cooking time: 30 minutes • Serves: 2-4

Ingredients

2 onions	125 ml (4 fl oz) red wine
2 cloves garlic	5 ml (1 tsp) chopped fresh or dried thyme
30 ml (2 tbsp) sunflower oil	5 ml (1 tsp) chopped fresh or dried basil
250 g (9 oz) minced beef	300 g (10½ oz) spaghetti
Salt and freshly ground black pepper	15 ml (1 tbsp) olive oil
Ground paprika	Grated Parmesan cheese, to serve
500 g (1 1b 2 oz) canned tomatoes	Fresh herb sprigs, to garnish
85 g (3 oz) tomato purée	

Method

1

Peel the onions and garlic and finely chop. Heat the sunflower oil in a saucepan and cook the onion and garlic until softened.

2

Add the minced beef and cook for about 5 minutes, stirring. Season with salt and pepper and paprika.

3

Add the tomatoes, tomato purée and red wine, bring to the boil, then reduce the heat and cook for about 15 minutes, stirring occasionally, until the beef is cooked and tender. Add the thyme and basil towards the end of the cooking time.

4

Meanwhile, bring a large saucepan of lightly salted water to the boil and add the spaghetti and olive oil.
Cook for 8-10 minutes, or until al dente, stirring occasionally with a fork.

5

Drain the spaghetti and serve on warmed serving plates with the meat sauce spooned over. Sprinkle with grated Parmesan cheese before serving and garnish with fresh herb sprigs.

Serving suggestion
Serve with hot garlic and herb bread.

Variations
Use minced pork, lamb or chicken in place of beef. Use 3 leeks or 8 shallots in place of onions.
Use apple juice or beef stock in place of red wine.

Pasta with Leeks and Ham

Leeks and ham always combine well, and are especially delicious in this rich and creamy pasta sauce.

Preparation time: 15 minutes • Cooking time: 20 minutes • Serves: 4

Ingredients

250 g (9 oz) tagliatelle	150 ml (¼ pint) beef stock
Salt and freshly ground black pepper	50 ml (2 fl oz) double cream
15 ml (1 tbsp) olive oil	Grated nutmeg
500 g (1 1b 2 oz) leeks	200 g (7 oz) cooked lean ham

Method

1

Cook the pasta in a large saucepan of boiling, salted water with the oil for 8-12 minutes, or until al dente. Drain and keep warm.

2

Meanwhile, slice the leeks into rings, then wash thoroughly. Bring the stock to the boil in a saucepan.
Add the leeks, cover and cook gently for 15 minutes, stirring occasionally. After 5 minutes' cooking time,
add the cream and salt and pepper and grated nutmeg to taste.

3

Slice the ham into strips. Mix the pasta with the creamy leek sauce and ham, tossing together to mix well. Serve hot.

Serving suggestion
Serve with warm ciabatta.

Variations
Use onions in place of leeks. Use smoked ham for a change.

Pasta with Chicken and Shrimps

Make this interesting pasta dish with either pasta spirals or penne.

Preparation time: 15 minutes • Cooking time: 40 minutes • Serves: 4

Ingredients

450 g (1 lb) skinless, boneless chicken breasts	*25 g (1 oz) plain flour*
90 ml (6 tbsp) white wine	*300 ml (½ pint) single cream*
Salt and freshly ground black pepper	*15 ml (1 tbsp) chopped fresh dill*
175 g (6 oz) shelled broad beans	*Cooked pasta, to serve*
55 g (2 oz) potted shrimps	

Method

1

Cut the chicken breasts into strips about 2-cm (¾-in) wide. Place in a shallow ovenproof dish, pour over the wine and season with salt and pepper.

2

Cover and cook in a preheated oven at 180°C/350°F/Gas Mark 4 until cooked and tender.

3

Allow to cool, then cut the strips in half lengthways. Strain and reserve the cooking liquid.

4

Meanwhile, cook the beans in a saucepan of boiling water for about 5 minutes, until just tender, then drain and remove and discard the white outer skins. If you use defrosted frozen broad beans, the skins can be slipped off before cooking, since the beans have already been blanched.

5

Melt the potted shrimps in a saucepan over a gentle heat, then stir in the flour and blend carefully. Continue cooking for 1-2 minutes, stirring continuously.

6

Make the single cream up to 425 ml (¾ pint) using the reserved cooking liquid. Off the heat, stir into the floured shrimps and return to a low heat, stirring continuously, until a smooth sauce is formed.

7

Add the dill and the shelled beans and season to taste with salt and pepper. Stir in the chicken strips, heat gently until hot and serve immediately with hot pasta.

Serving suggestion
Serve with a green side salad.

Variations
This recipe can be made with ready-cooked chicken, or use cooked ham. Use sweetcorn kernels in place of broad beans – they will require no precooking.

Chinese Noodles with Vegetables

This is an Oriental-inspired vegetarian noodle dish. Chinese noodles are mixed with bamboo shoots, black mushrooms and cucumber and a light sauce consisting of a reduction of the cooking juices.

Preparation time: 40 minutes • Cooking time: 20 minutes • Serves: 4-6

Ingredients

10 g (¼ oz) dried black Chinese mushrooms	400 g (14 oz) Chinese noodles
2.5-cm (1-in) piece fresh ginger root	Salt and freshly ground black pepper
1 clove garlic	45 ml (3 tbsp) olive oil
2 carrots	1 small chilli
¼ cucumber	75 ml (5 tbsp) soy sauce
225 g (8 oz) bamboo shoots	15 ml (1 tbsp) honey
115 g (4 oz) bean sprouts	Chopped fresh chives, to garnish

Method

1
Soak the mushrooms in a bowl, covered with hot water, for 15 minutes. Trim off the sandy stumps, then boil the mushrooms in a saucepan of water for 5 minutes.

2
Peel the ginger and garlic and finely chop. Set aside.

3
Peel the carrots and cut into matchsticks. Squeeze out the water from the mushrooms and slice into matchsticks. Set aside.

4
Peel and slice the cucumber into matchsticks. Set aside.

5
Trim the bamboo shoots and cut into slices, then into matchsticks. Blanch in a pan of boiling water for 2 minutes. Set aside to drain thoroughly.

6
Trim and wash the bean sprouts. Blanch for 1 minute in a pan of boiling water. Plunge into cold water and set aside to drain thoroughly.

7
Cook the noodles in a pan of boiling, salted water for a few minutes, following the instructions on the packet. Drain, rinse and set aside to drain thoroughly.

8
In a frying pan, heat the oil and fry the ginger, garlic and chilli for for 30 seconds, stirring.

9
Add the bamboo shoots, mushrooms and carrots. Fry for 4 minutes, then add the bean sprouts. Cook for another 2 minutes, stirring occasionally.

10
Add the noodles, soy sauce and honey. Stir well and cook until heated through, stirring.

11
Add the cucumber and seasoning and heat for 1 minute, stirring. Remove and discard the chilli. Serve immediately garnished with chopped chives.

Serving suggestion
Serve with fresh crusty bread or bread rolls.

Variations
Use sliced courgettes in place of bean sprouts. Use parsnips in place of carrots.

Spaghetti with Pine Nuts

This crunchy, flavoursome combination makes good use of convenience ingredients often found in the store cupboard.

Preparation time: 15 minutes • Cooking time: 25 minutes • Serves: 4

Ingredients

350 g (12 oz) spaghetti	*1 clove garlic, crushed*
Salt and freshly ground black pepper	*25 g (1 oz) chopped fresh parsley*
15 ml (1 tbsp) sunflower oil	*115 g (4 oz) pine nuts*
90 ml (3 fl oz) olive oil	*400-g (14-oz) can artichoke hearts, drained and chopped*
1 large onion, sliced	*55 g (2 oz) Cheddar cheese, grated (optional)*

Method

1

Cook the pasta in a large saucepan of lightly salted, boiling water with the sunflower oil added for 8-12 minutes, or until al dente. Drain and keep warm.

2

Heat the olive oil in a frying pan. Add the onion and garlic and cook for 5 minutes, stirring occasionally.

3

Add the parsley, pine nuts and artichokes and cook gently for 5 minutes, stirring occasionally.

4

Stir in the cooked pasta and reheat gently, stirring occasionally. Season to taste with salt and pepper.

5

Just before serving, stir in the grated cheese, if using, and serve immediately.

Serving suggestion

Serve with a mixed dark leaf side salad.

Variations

Use tagliatelle or fettuccine in place of spaghetti. Use Parmesan cheese in place of Cheddar. Use fresh basil in place of parsley.

Spinach-Stuffed Cannelloni

The filling for this appetising cannelloni dish combines Mozzarella cheese and ham with spinach.

Preparation time: 30 minutes • Cooking time: 15 minutes • Serves: 4

Ingredients

12 cannelloni	3 slices ham, cut into thin strips
Salt and freshly ground black pepper	225 g (8 oz) Mozzarella cheese, cut into small cubes
25 g (1 oz) butter	300 ml (½ pint) béchamel sauce (page 48)
225 g (8 oz) fresh spinach, washed and finely shredded	A pinch of ground nutmeg
	45 ml (3 tbsp) grated Parmesan cheese

Method

1
Cook the cannelloni in a large saucepan of lightly salted, boiling water for about 3 minutes, removing when still quite firm. Rinse in hot water and set aside to drain on a slightly damp tea-towel.

2
Heat the butter in a frying pan, add the spinach and ham and cook gently for 2 minutes, stirring.

3
Remove the pan from the heat and stir in the Mozzarella cheese.

4
Fill each of the cannelloni with the spinach filling.

5
Lay the cannelloni in a lightly greased ovenproof dish, pour over the béchamel sauce and season with nutmeg and salt and pepper.

6
Sprinkle over the Parmesan cheese and bake in a preheated oven at 220°C/425°F/Gas Mark 7 for about 15 minutes, until piping hot and bubbling. Serve immediately.

Serving suggestions
Serve with fresh cooked vegetables, such as baby carrots and courgettes, or a mixed salad and crusty bread.

Variations
Use mild Cheddar cheese in place of Mozzarella. Use cooked chicken or turkey in place of ham.

Cook's tip
The topping should be lightly golden when cooked. If necessary, place under a hot grill for 1-2 minutes before serving.

Fresh Pasta with Basil and Tomato Sauce

Fresh pasta with lots of finely chopped basil is combined with a cooked tomato sauce
in this delectable and filling dish.

Preparation time: 10 minutes • Cooking time: 25 minutes • Serves: 4

Ingredients

450 g (1 1b) fresh pasta	*3 tomatoes, skinned, seeded and chopped*
Salt and freshly ground black pepper	*10 fresh basil leaves, finely chopped*
45 ml (3 tbsp) olive oil	*Fresh basil sprigs, to garnish*
1 clove garlic, chopped	

Method

1

Cook the pasta in a large saucepan of lightly salted, boiling water for 3-4 minutes, or until al dente.
Rinse under hot water and set aside to drain. Keep warm.

2

Heat the olive oil in a frying pan and cook the garlic, tomatoes and salt and pepper over a gentle heat
for 10-15 minutes, stirring frequently.

3

Stir the drained pasta into the sauce, mix well and heat through for a few minutes, stirring.

4

Just before serving, stir in the finely chopped basil. Check and adjust the seasoning and serve hot,
garnished with fresh basil sprigs.

Serving suggestion

Serve with a green salad and hot garlic bread.

Variations

Add a finely chopped onion to the olive oil with the garlic, allow it to brown slightly, then add the tomatoes and continue
cooking as above. Use fresh parsley, tarragon or coriander in place of basil. Use chilli or herb oil in place of olive oil.

Cook's tip

Use really ripe tomatoes for this recipe, for the best flavour.

Spaghetti with Courgette Sauce

A flavourful vegetarian dish which is quick and very easy to prepare.

Preparation time: 20 minutes • Cooking time: 15 minutes • Serves: 2-4

Ingredients

300 g (10½ oz) spaghetti	500 g (1 1b 2 oz) courgettes
Salt and freshly ground black pepper	30 ml (2 tbsp) chopped fresh mixed herbs
75 ml (5 tbsp) olive oil	125 ml (4 fl oz) double cream
1 onion	1 beefsteak tomato, skinned
2 cloves garlic	

Method

1

Place the spaghetti in a saucepan of boiling salted water with 15 ml (1 tbsp) oil added, and cook for about 8-10 minutes, or until al dente, stirring occasionally with a fork. Drain well, set aside and keep warm.

2

Meanwhile, to make the courgette sauce, peel and thinly slice the onion and garlic, and slice the courgettes into strips.

3

Heat the remaining oil in a frying pan, add the onion, garlic and courgettes and cook for about 3 minutes, stirring occasionally.

4

Add the herbs and simmer for a further minute before adding the cream and salt and pepper.

5

Cut the tomato into chunks and add to the pan. Heat through briefly until piping hot, stirring occasionally.

6

Serve the hot spaghetti with the courgette sauce spooned over the top.

Serving suggestion

Serve with thick slices of fresh wholemeal bread.

Variations

Use 2 leeks in place of the onion. Use mushrooms in place of all or half the courgettes. Use 2 plum tomatoes in place of the beefsteak tomato. Sprinkle with grated Parmesan or Cheddar cheese just before serving, if you like.

Herb Ravioli with Chicken Stock

Homemade ravioli dough is coated with fresh herbs and cooked in a chicken stock flavoured with rosemary.
This delicious recipe is a soup and pasta dish in one.

Preparation time: 45 minutes • Cooking time: 10 minutes • Serves: 4

Ingredients

175 g (6 oz) plain flour, sifted	*1 bunch of fresh parsley, washed and chopped*
Salt and freshly ground black pepper	*1 litre (1¾ pints) chicken stock*
1 egg, beaten	*5 ml (1 tsp) dried rosemary*
1 bunch of fresh chervil, washed and chopped	

Method

1

Make the dough by mixing together the flour, a good pinch of salt and the egg in a large bowl. Set aside to rest for 30 minutes.

2

Pass the dough through a pasta machine, flouring both sides of the dough as it goes through the rollers to prevent sticking. Cut the dough into long strips. Alternatively, roll out the dough thinly using a rolling pin and cut into strips.

3

Spread out half of the strips onto a clean work surface and sprinkle over the chervil and parsley.

4

Place the remaining strips on top, press down well all along the strips with your fingers and then once again run the strips through the rollers of the pasta machine, or roll with a rolling pin.

5

Heat the stock and rosemary together in a saucepan until just boiling. Season with salt and pepper.

6

Cut the dough into the desired ravioli shapes.

7

Cook the ravioli in the boiling stock for approximately 2-4 minutes. Serve very hot in shallow soup bowls.

Serving suggestion

Serve with fresh crusty French bread or toast.

Variations

Other fresh herbs such as chives, basil, marjoram and tarragon can be used instead of the chervil and parsley. Use vegetable stock in place of chicken stock for a vegetarian option.

Cook's tip

The herbs should be visible through the pasta. Pass the sandwiched strips of dough through closely-set rollers on the pasta machine, if using.

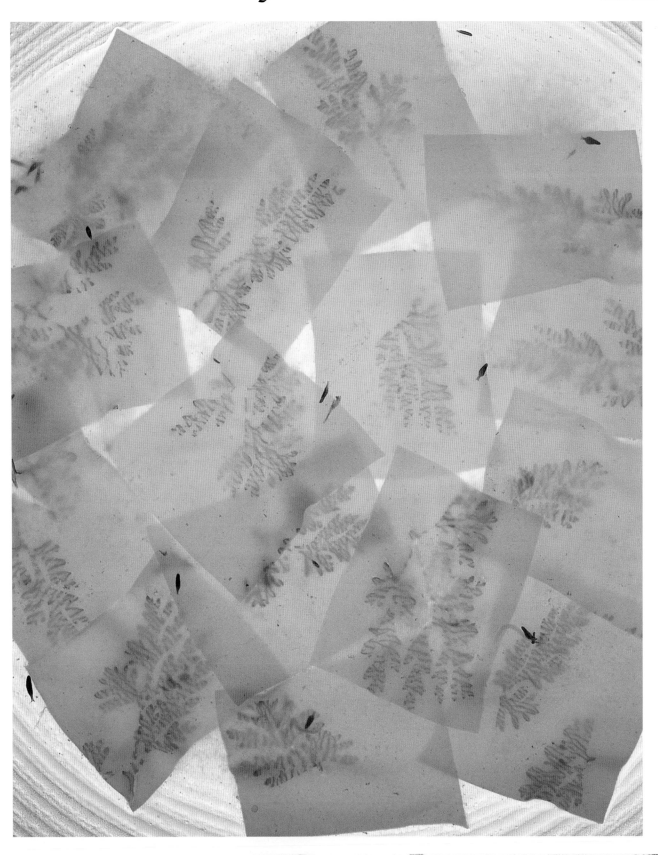

Fresh Pasta with Garlic and Parsley

This is a very simple pasta dish, but no less enjoyable for that. Use fresh flat-leafed parsley for this recipe, if it is available.

Preparation time: 10 minutes • Cooking time: 10 minutes • Serves: 4

Ingredients

450 g (1 1b) fresh pasta	*A few drops of olive oil*
Salt and freshly ground black pepper	*30 ml (2 tbsp) finely chopped parsley*
55 g (2 oz) butter	*Fresh herb sprigs, to garnish*
2 cloves garlic, finely chopped	

Method

1

Cook the pasta in a large saucepan of lightly salted, boiling water for 3-4 minutes, or until al dente. Rinse in hot water and set aside to drain. Keep warm.

2

Melt the butter in a frying pan, add the garlic and fry for 1 minute.

3

Add the drained pasta to the pan, stirring well to mix in the garlic. Cook for a few minutes, stirring.

4

Add a few drops of olive oil to the pan, remove from the heat and sprinkle over the chopped parsley. Season with salt and pepper and serve immediately, garnished with fresh herb sprigs.

Serving suggestion

Serve with stir-fried mixed shredded vegetables.

Variations

If preferred, the butter may be substituted with olive oil. Use chopped fresh mixed herbs or coriander in place of parsley.

Cook's tip

Mix together the butter, garlic and parsley. Keep in the refrigerator and use for this dish when unexpected guests arrive.

Pasta with Fresh Basil Sauce

The fresh basil sauce in this recipe is made by pounding basil leaves with garlic, Parmesan cheese
and olive oil using a pestle and mortar.

Preparation time: 25 minutes • Cooking time: 8 minutes • Serves: 4

Ingredients

450 g (1 1b) fresh pasta	*30 ml (2 tbsp) grated fresh Parmesan cheese*
Salt and freshly ground black pepper	*50 ml (2 fl oz) olive oil*
20 fresh basil leaves	*25 g (1 oz) butter*
1 clove garlic	*Fresh basil sprigs, to garnish*

Method

1
Cook the pasta in salted, boiling water. Drain, rinse, then set aside to drain well.

2
Pound the basil leaves with a mortar and pestle, then add the garlic and pound until well blended.

3
Add the Parmesan cheese and continue to pound.

4
Transfer the basil mixture to a large bowl, whisk in the olive oil, then set aside.

5
Place cooked pasta in a large pan, add the butter and toss to mix. Place the pan over a gentle heat and add the basil sauce.
Season with salt and pepper and heat through, stirring continuously with a wooden spoon.
When hot, serve immediately garnished with basil sprigs.

Serving suggestion
Serve with a mixed leaf salad and slices of ciabatta.

Variations
The sauce can be made in a food processor by adding all the ingredients together and processing until smooth. This reduces the
preparation time to about 3 minutes. Sprinkle a handful of pine nuts over the pasta before serving, if you like.

Conchiglie with Two Sauces

This exciting pasta recipe offers two contrasting vegetable sauces – tomato and mushroom – in a single dish.

Preparation time: 20 minutes • Cooking time: 30 minutes • Serves: 4

Ingredients

For the tomato sauce	For the mushroom sauce
1 large onion, very finely chopped	250 g (9 oz) oyster mushrooms
5 ml (1 tsp) bouillon or stock powder	25 g (1 oz) butter
1 clove garlic, crushed	1 vegetable stock cube, crumbled
2.5 ml (½ tsp) dried thyme	60 ml (4 tbsp) fromage frais
A pinch of dried rosemary	450 g (1 1b) cooked conchiglie (pasta shells)
400-g (14-oz) can tomatoes	Chopped, fresh parsley, to garnish

Method

1

To make the tomato sauce, place the onion, bouillon powder, 45 ml (3 tbsp) water and garlic in a pan and cook very gently for 7-10 minutes, or until the onion is soft, stirring occasionally.

2

Add the thyme and rosemary and cook for 1 minute, stirring.

3

Chop the tomatoes and add to the pan together with the tomato juice.

4

Bring to the boil and boil rapidly until the sauce has reduced and thickened, stirring occasionally.

5

Meanwhile, make the mushroom sauce. Finely chop the mushrooms. Melt the butter in a pan and add the mushrooms and stock cube.

6

Simmer very gently for 10-15 minutes, stirring occasionally. Remove the pan from the heat and stir in the fromage frais. Heat gently until hot, but do not allow to boil.

7

Divide the hot pasta between 4 serving dishes and pour the tomato sauce over one half of the pasta and the mushroom sauce over the other half of the pasta.

8

Sprinkle the chopped parsley over the two sauces and serve at once.

Serving suggestion
Serve with a chopped mixed garden salad and fresh bread rolls.

Variations
Use button mushrooms in place of the oyster mushrooms. Use crème fraîche in place of fromage frais.

Cook's tip
The sauces can be prepared in advance, refrigerated and reheated thoroughly when required.

Spaghetti with Asparagus

Tender asparagus spears are combined with ham, eggs and cheese in this tasty spaghetti dish.

Preparation time: 20 minutes • Cooking time: 20 minutes • Serves: 4

Ingredients

500 g (1 1b 2 oz) asparagus	*1 clove garlic*
Salt	*250 g (9 oz) piece of boiled ham*
A pinch of sugar	*15 ml (1 tbsp) butter*
400 g (14 oz) spaghetti	*3 eggs*
1 onion	*100 g (3½ oz) fresh Parmesan cheese, grated*

Method

1
Peel the stalks of the asparagus, removing and discarding any woody parts of the stems. Slice into small pieces.

2
Place the asparagus in a large saucepan of lightly salted, boiling water with the sugar added.
Cook for about 10-15 minutes, or until the asparagus is tender, then drain, set aside and keep warm.

3
Cook the spaghetti in a large saucepan of lightly salted, boiling water for about 10 minutes, or until al dente.
Drain, set aside and keep warm.

4
Peel the onion and garlic and thinly slice. Cut the ham into cubes and set aside.

5
Melt the butter in a pan and cook the onion and garlic until softened, stirring occasionally.

6
Lightly beat the eggs with the Parmesan cheese and mix in the ham. Add the egg mixture to the onions in the pan.

7
Use a spatula to stir the egg mixture until lightly cooked, to prevent it sticking to the pan.

8
Mix the ham and egg mixture with the asparagus and stir into the spaghetti. Serve immediately.

Serving suggestion
Serve with hot garlic and herb bread.

Variations
Use Cheddar or Gruyère cheese in place of Parmesan cheese. Use pasta spirals or shapes in place of spaghetti.

Cook's tip
When buying asparagus, choose straight, firm and evenly sized spears which are bright in colour.
The tips should be tightly budded.

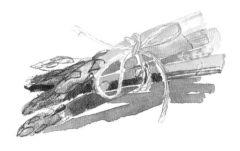

Index